THE BROWN LADY

THE GHOST OF RAYNHAM HALL

BY MEGAN COOLEY PETERSON

CAPSTONE PRESS
a capstone imprint

Snap Books are published by Capstone Press, an imprint of Capstone.
1710 Roe Crest Drive,
North Mankato, Minnesota 56003
www.capstonepub.com

Library of Congress Cataloging-in-Publication Data is available
on the Library of Congress website.

ISBN: 978-1-5435-7340-4 (hardcover)
ISBN: 978-1-4966-6613-0 (paperback)
ISBN: 978-1-5435-7349-7 (eBook PDF)

Summary: A ghostly woman in a brown dress has been repeatedly sighted in a
centuries-old mansion in Norfolk, England. Many believe the Brown Lady of Raynham Hall
is the spirit of Lady Dorothy Walpole, wife of Charles Townsend. According to legend, Charles
became upset with Dorothy and locked her inside Raynham Hall until she died.
To this day, her ghost still allegedly wanders the home.

Editorial Credits
Editor: Eliza Leahy; Designers: Lori Bye and Brann Garvey; Media Researcher: Tracy Cummins;
Production Specialist: Kathy McColley

Image Credits
Alamy: Art Collection 2, 5, ASP Religion, 24, Major Gilbert, 29, Mike Booth, 8; Bridgeman
Images: Look and Learn, 17, Look and Learn/Elgar Collection, 7, The Marsden Archive, UK/
Photo © Simon Marsden, 23, 27; Getty Images: Bettmann, 21, Time Life Pictures/David E.
Scherman, 22, Time Life Pictures/The LIFE Picture Collection, 18; iStockphoto: Renphoto,
Cover, smpering, 15; Newscom: The Print Collector Heritage Images, 13; Shutterstock:
avtk, Design Element, Chantal de Bruijne, Design Element, Evgeniia Litovchenko, 11,
Giraphics, Design Element, GoMixer, Design Element, MagicDogWorkshop, Design Element,
NikhomTreeVector, Design Element, sloukam, 9; Shutterstock Premier: Tony O'Rahilly, 25

Direct Quotations
page 10: Crain, Mary Beth. *Haunted Christmas: Yuletide Ghosts and Other Spooky
Holiday Happenings.* Guilford, CT: Globe Pequot Press, 2010, 36.
page 14: Marryat, Florence. *There Is No Death.* London: Kegan Paul, Trench,
Trübner & Co., Ltd., 1891, 8.
pages 16, 19: http://www.xenophon.org.uk/indreshira.html

All internet sites appearing in front and back matter were available and accurate
when this book was sent to press.

Printed and bound in the USA. PA99

TABLE OF CONTENTS

A HAUNTED MANSION

At the end of a long drive in Norfolk, England, sits Raynham Hall. This large stone mansion has stood for 400 years. For centuries it has been home to the Townshends, a **noble** English family. It may still be home to the ghost of Dorothy Walpole, who died there in 1726. Some say she was murdered within its walls.

One of the world's most famous ghost photos was taken at Raynham Hall in 1936. Photographers noticed something strange on the grand staircase. They snapped a few photos. When they developed the film, they were shocked by what they saw—a hazy white figure descending the stairs. Was it Dorothy's ghost? A smudge on the film? **Skeptics** believe the photo was faked. Or is there some other explanation?

FACT

The ghosts of a cocker spaniel and a duke are also said to haunt Raynham Hall.

Dorothy Walpole was born in Norfolk, England, on September 18, 1686.

CHAPTER ONE

LOCKED AWAY

According to **legend,** Lady Dorothy Walpole had been in love with Charles Townshend since childhood. Charles came from a wealthy family. He lived his entire life at Raynham Hall. But Dorothy's father had not allowed the young couple to marry. He served as Charles's guardian. He worried their marriage would give the appearance that he was using his **guardianship** over Charles for his own gain. So Charles wed another woman.

Dorothy and Charles's love story did not end, however. After his first wife died, Charles married Dorothy in 1713. They lived together at Raynham Hall and had seven children together. They appeared to have a perfect marriage.

But Dorothy had kept a secret from her husband.

Construction began on Raynham Hall in the 1620s. The estate covers 7,000 acres.

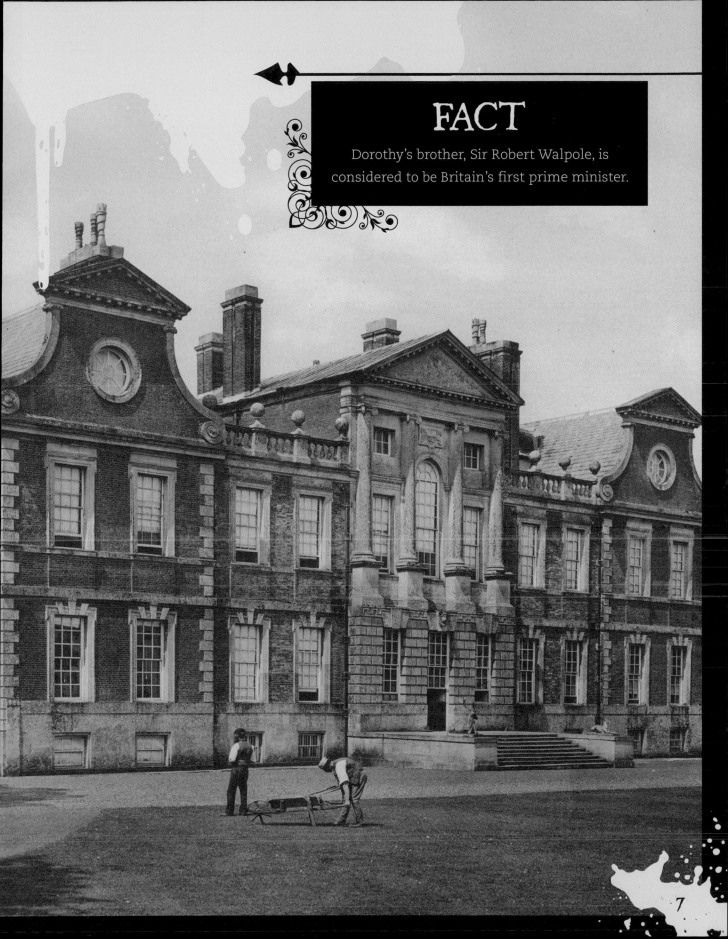

FACT

Dorothy's brother, Sir Robert Walpole, is considered to be Britain's first prime minister.

While Charles was married to his first wife, Dorothy **allegedly** had a secret romance with another man. Unmarried women of noble birth were not allowed to have secret romances. If anyone found out, Dorothy's **reputation** may have been ruined. So Dorothy kept her past a secret.

On March 29, 1726, tragedy struck Raynham Hall. Lady Dorothy died. The official story is that she died of smallpox. This disease can cause a fever, rash, blisters, and even death. She was buried at Saint Mary's Church in Raynham Park.

Soon, a darker rumor about the end of Dorothy's life began to swirl. Charles had allegedly learned of Dorothy's love affair. In a rage, he locked his wife in her rooms inside Raynham Hall. He kept her from her children and the outside world. Some stories say Dorothy died of a broken heart. Another story says Charles pushed his wife down the oak grand staircase, killing her.

Whatever had happened, Lady Dorothy's story was far from over.

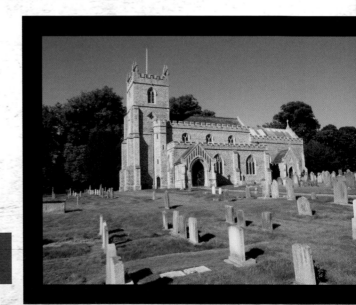

The church where Lady Dorothy was buried, Saint Mary's Church, was rebuilt in the 1860s.

WINDSOR CASTLE

Windsor Castle in England is also said to be haunted. Queen Elizabeth I allegedly haunts the library. The sound of her walking through the room in high heels can be heard. Then her figure suddenly appears before passing through the wall. The sound of dragging chains is thought to be caused by the ghost of King Henry VIII.

CHAPTER TWO

THE LADY OF THE HOUSE RETURNS

By 1786, Raynham Hall had a new master. George Townshend, Charles's grandson, was known for throwing fancy parties at the mansion. He was said to invite his guests to view the ghost of Dorothy Walpole. Some guests claimed they saw her ghost carrying a lantern down the hallways. Her ghost wore a brown dress, which earned her the nickname the Brown Lady.

ROYALLY TERRIFIED

In 1815, Raynham Hall hosted the future king of England. George IV was sleeping one night when he was startled awake. A pale woman stood at the end of his bed. She wore a brown dress. "I will not spend another hour in this **accursed** house, for tonight I have seen that which I hope to God I never see again," he said. George left and vowed never to return. Had he seen Dorothy's ghost?

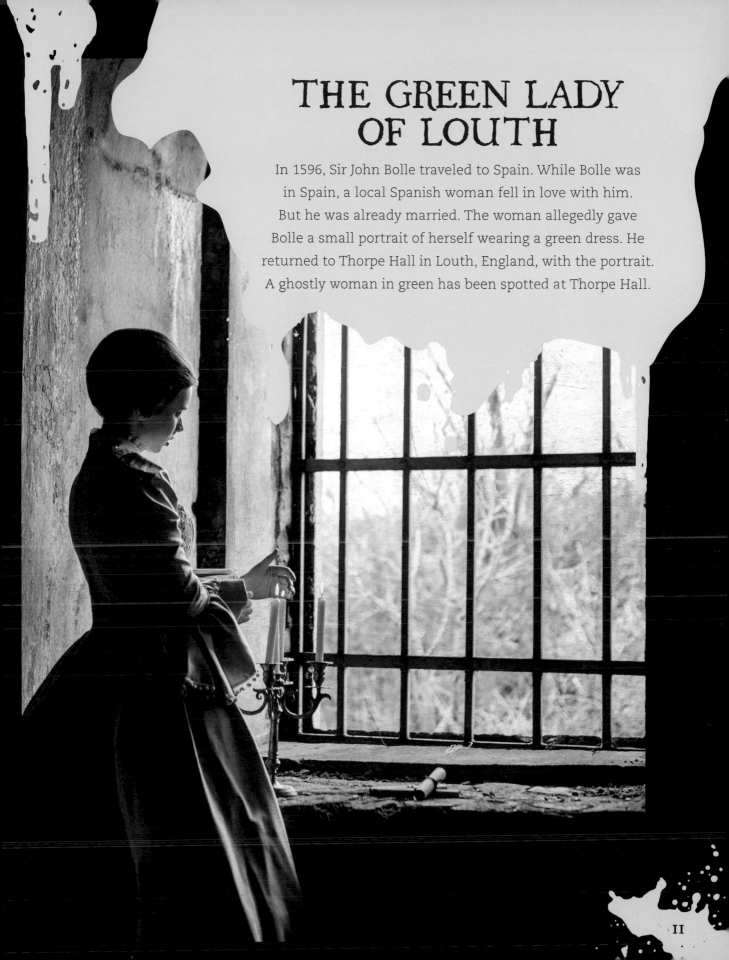

THE GREEN LADY
OF LOUTH

In 1596, Sir John Bolle traveled to Spain. While Bolle was in Spain, a local Spanish woman fell in love with him. But he was already married. The woman allegedly gave Bolle a small portrait of herself wearing a green dress. He returned to Thorpe Hall in Louth, England, with the portrait. A ghostly woman in green has been spotted at Thorpe Hall.

A CHRISTMAS HAUNTING

Christmas 1835 was anything but merry at Raynham Hall. Colonel Loftus arrived at Raynham to spend the holiday with family. But when Loftus arrived, he got much more than holiday cheer. Loftus claimed he saw Lady Dorothy's ghost on the staircase, carrying a lamp. He said the ghost had dark holes where its eyes should be.

SKEPTIC'S NOTE

People visiting supposed haunted houses may go in expecting a ghostly encounter. They blame everyday noises or images on ghosts because they want to.

A HAUNTED PORTRAIT

Not long after Christmas, a new Lord and Lady Townshend moved into Raynham Hall. They redecorated the mansion and bought new furniture. When they arrived at the hall with friends, rumors spread that the house was haunted. A painting of Lady Dorothy hung in one of the bedrooms. In the portrait, she wore a brown dress with ruffles around her neck. Guests and servants claimed they saw the woman from the painting wandering around the house. Their guests and workers began to flee.

Lord Townshend told his friend Frederick Marryat about the troubles at the Hall. Marryat did not believe the Hall was haunted. He volunteered to spend three nights in the bedroom where the painting hung.

Frederick Marryat was a retired naval officer and a popular author of children's books and adventure novels.

On the first night he stayed in the bedroom, Marryat tucked a loaded pistol under his pillow and went to bed. But no ghostly figure appeared. The second night passed without a ghostly sighting. On the third night, Lord Townshend's nephews knocked on Marryat's door. They wanted to show him a new gun that had come in from London. Marryat grabbed his pistol and went to their room to see the gun. After looking at the gun, he turned to leave. The young men said they would go with him "in case you meet the Brown Lady." They laughed as they walked back down the darkened hallway.

Suddenly, a woman carrying a lighted lamp appeared at the far end of the hall. Marryat hid behind a hallway door. As the woman passed by, Marryat's heart leaped into his throat—she was the woman from the painting! Marryat put his finger on the pistol's trigger. He was about to call out to the ghost when it stopped, turned around, and held the lamp to its face. The ghost flashed a sinister grin at Marryat. Terrified, Marryat aimed his pistol and fired at the ghost. The ghost vanished, and the bullet lodged in one of the heavy wooden doors.

A GHOSTLY PARTY

A man named Charles Loftus reported that in 1842, the Brown
Lady appeared at Raynham during a party. When the guests
decided to dance, one of the women went upstairs to her room.
She wanted to wear her fancy white gloves. As she walked up the
stairs, she came face-to-face with the ghost of Lady Dorothy. She
stared at the ghost, which suddenly faded away. Was the woman
imagining things? Or had she really seen a ghost?

CHAPTER THREE

CATCHING THE BROWN LADY ON FILM

In 1936, Lady Gwladys Townshend allowed two photographers to photograph Raynham Hall. Indre Shira and Captain Hubert Provand arrived early on the morning of September 19. Around eight in the morning, they began snapping photos of the grounds and the home's interior.

At four in the afternoon, they set up their camera in front of the oak staircase. This was the same staircase Charles Townshend had allegedly pushed Dorothy down. As Provand took a practice shot, Shira flashed the light. Provand focused the camera for a second shot. Shira waited with the **flashbulb** ready, his gaze rising up the grand staircase. He noticed a hazy, veiled figure floating down the stairs. "Quick! Quick!" he called out to Provand. "There's something! Are you ready?"

The interior of Raynham Hall was updated by architect William Kent starting in 1725.

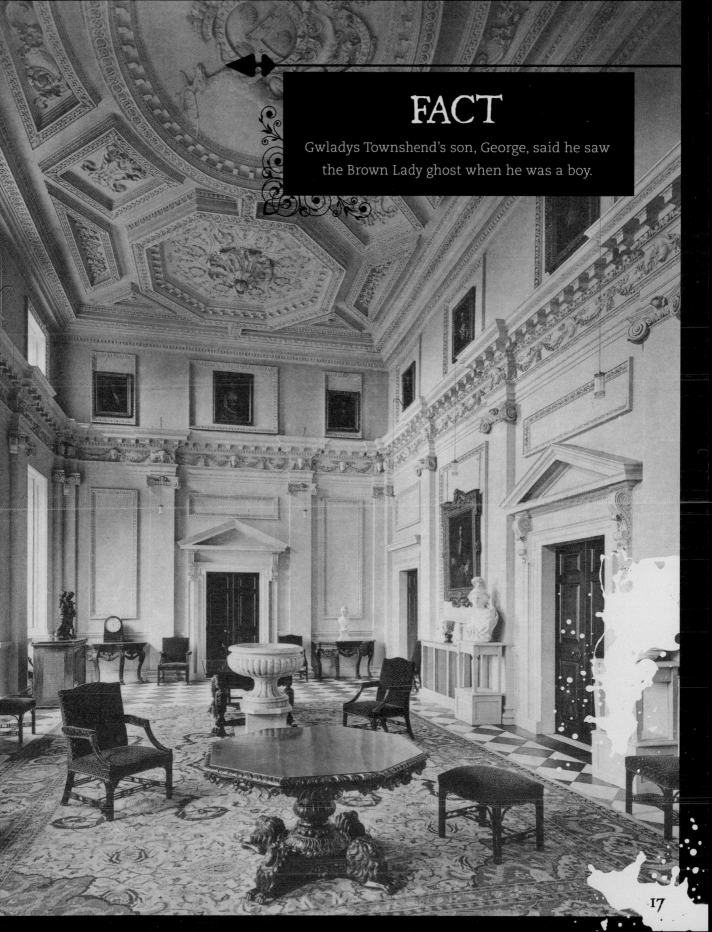

FACT

Gwladys Townshend's son, George, said he saw the Brown Lady ghost when he was a boy.

The famous photo of the Brown Lady was also
published overseas in *Life* magazine in January 1937.

Provand removed the lens cap and snapped the photo just as Shira flashed the light. After taking the photo, Shira explained what he had seen. Provand dismissed him, assuming he must have imagined it. They packed up their gear and left Raynham Hall.

Provand and Shira soon began developing the photos they took at Raynham. As they developed the **negative** of the staircase, the men leaned in close. "Good Lord!" Provand said. "There's something on the staircase negative after all!" The glowing figure Shira had seen on the stairs appeared. It seemed to be gliding down the staircase. Had the Brown Lady just been captured on film? They quickly published the photo in *Country Life* magazine.

SPIRITUALISM

Spiritualism became popular in the 1800s. Mediums claimed they could connect people to loved ones who had died. They often held **séances** around a table. Sometimes the table would move, or something would knock against it. People believed their loved ones were trying to speak with them. But many mediums were later exposed as frauds. They knocked the tables and made them move.

CHAPTER FOUR

OTHER FAMOUS GHOST PHOTOS

The Brown Lady ghost photograph appeared in the December 1936 issue of *Country Life* magazine. The photo soon spread around the world, appearing in countless books and magazines. Many people believed the photo proved ghosts were real. And many other supposed ghost photos exist.

AMITYVILLE GHOST PHOTO

In 1975, the Lutz family moved into a large home on Ocean Avenue in Amityville, New York. Brutal murders had taken place in the house only the year before. Ronald DeFeo Jr. shot his parents and younger siblings while they slept. Since no one else wanted the house, the Lutzes bought it at a bargain.

After living in the home for only 28 days, the Lutz family fled. They claimed the house was haunted. In February 1976, **paranormal** investigators Ed and Lorraine Warren came to the house. Their photographer, Gene Campbell, set up his camera on the second-floor landing. It snapped photos during the night. One photo appears to show a young boy peering out of a doorway. Some people believe it is the ghost of John DeFeo. John was only nine years old when he was killed.

Ed and Lorraine Warren were the founders of the New England Society for Psychic Research.

SKEPTIC'S NOTE

The Lutzes have been accused of faking the hauntings.
George Lutz held onto the photo for three years.
He revealed it on a TV talk show.

BORLEY RECTORY'S FLOATING BRICK

The Borley **Rectory** was once considered England's most haunted house. Built in 1862 or 1863, the building housed religious leaders of the local church. It was built on the site of an old **monastery**. Witnesses said they saw a ghostly nun roaming the property. Objects moved on their own. Some said they even saw a headless ghost walk through some bushes.

The Borley Rectory burned down in 1939. On April 5, 1944, ghost hunter Harry Price and a photographer from *Life* magazine arrived at Borley. A crew was already on-site, tearing down the ruins. Price was writing an article about haunted places in England. As the photographer snapped photos, a brick suddenly shot up into the air. The photographer captured a photo of the brick in midair. Price wondered if they had just seen **poltergeist** activity. He claimed there were no workers near that part of the house when the brick flew.

New owners of the rectory accidentally caused the fire in 1939, leaving the building in ruins.

HARRY PRICE

Harry Price was one of the first ghost hunters. He gained fame
in the 1930s when he investigated the hauntings at Borley.
He moved into the house and wrote a book about the ghostly
activity he witnessed. Many people disputed Price's findings.
Some even said he made up the haunting. One witness said
Price kept bricks and pebbles in his pockets. Price would
allegedly throw them and pretend it was ghostly activity.

SKEPTIC'S NOTE

Journalist Cynthia Ledsham was also with Harry Price and
the photographer in 1944. She said workers were throwing
bricks near where the photo was taken.

PHANTOM MONK OF NEWBY

In 1963, Reverend Kenneth Lord visited Newby Church in Yorkshire, England. He took a photograph of the church's altar. When Lord developed his photo of the altar, he was shocked by what he found. A tall figure in a long, black robe stood on the altar. Its ghostly face seemed to be drooping or melting. Lord didn't see the figure when he took the photo. Some believe the ghost of a monk can be seen in the photograph.

FACT

The figure in the Newby Church photo is estimated to be 9 feet (2.7 meters) tall.

Newby Church was constructed in the 1870s. Prior to the Phantom Monk, there had been no documented paranormal events.

O'Rahilly's photo was shared on news outlets around the world.

WEM GHOST PHOTO

Smoke billowed from the town hall of Wem, Shropshire, England, in November 1995. As the 90-year-old building burned, Tony O'Rahilly joined a crowd across the street. He enjoyed photography and snapped a few photos of the blaze. After O'Rahilly developed the photo, he saw the figure of a girl standing in the flames. She wore an old-fashioned bonnet and dress. O'Rahilly believed he had captured the ghost of a little girl on film. His photograph became famous.

In 2010, a man named Brian Lear was reading the *Shropshire Star*. A postcard from Wem in 1922 was reprinted inside. The postcard showed a little girl wearing a bonnet and dress. She looked exactly like the girl from O'Rahilly's photo. Many people believe O'Rahilly used the image of the girl from the postcard to fake his photo. Tony O'Rahilly died in 2005. He maintained the photograph was never altered.

CHAPTER FIVE

IS THE BROWN LADY A REAL GHOST?

Many consider the photograph of the Brown Lady of Raynham Hall the most famous ghost photo ever taken. The hazy outline of a woman walking down the staircase has captivated viewers since 1936. But is the Brown Lady photo a real ghost photo? And does the ghost of Lady Dorothy Walpole really haunt Raynham Hall?

Photographers Hubert Provand and Indre Shira claimed they did nothing to alter the photograph. When they were developing the film, they invited Benjamin Jones to their darkroom. Jones worked as a chemist in a shop below their studio. Jones entered the room just as the negative was removed from the developer solution. Jones saw the ghostly figure and believed the negative had not been tampered with.

Since the famous photograph was published, there have been very few claims of haunting at Raynham Hall.

SKEPTIC'S NOTE

Some skeptics say the photograph doesn't show a ghost at all. They believe a **double exposure** produced the ghostlike shape.

The Society for Psychical Research investigated the Brown Lady photo in 1937. They concluded a faulty camera caused the white shape. But they never officially published their findings.

Lady Gwladys Townshend had yet another **theory**. She was religious and kept a **chapel** underneath the staircase. She believed the figure in the photograph was the Virgin Mary, not the Brown Lady.

No recent sightings of the Brown Lady have been reported. We may never know if the Brown Lady photo is real or was faked. But it can be fun to wonder if the ghost of Lady Dorothy Walpole still roams Raynham Hall.

FACT

Gwladys Townshend allegedly saw the Brown Lady more than once. She even contributed to a book called *True Ghost Stories*.

HOPING FOR GHOSTS?

Gwladys Townshend claimed she never invited Shira and Provand to photograph Raynham Hall. She said Shira approached her and asked if he could spend the night. He hoped to capture a photo of a ghost. Gwladys told him to come during the day when the house was open to the public.

Today, Raynham Hall is owned by Charles and Alison Townshend.

GLOSSARY

accursed (uh-KURST)—being under or as if under a curse

allegedly (uh-LEDGE-id-lee)—said to be true or to have happened, but without proof

chapel (CHAP-uhl)—a small room or space used for prayer or worship

double exposure (DUH-bul ik-SPO-zhur)—a photography method in which two photographs are taken on the same piece of film

flashbulb (FLASH-buhlb)—an electric bulb that can be used only once to produce a brief and very bright flash for taking photographs

guardianship (GAHR-dee-uhn-ship)—the position of being responsible for the care of someone, especially a child

legend (LEJ-uhnd)—a story passed down through the years that may not be completely true

monastery (MAH-nuh-ster-ee)—buildings where men live and study to devote themselves to their religious vows

negative (NEG-uh-tiv)—photographic image; prints can be made from negatives

noble (NOH-buhl)—belonging to a high social or political class

paranormal (pair-uh-NOR-muhl)—having to do with an unusual event that has no scientific explanation

poltergeist (POHL-tur-guyst)—a ghost that causes physical events, such as objects moving

rectory (REK-tuh-ree)—a house or building where church leaders live

reputation (rep-yuh-TAY-shuhn)—a person's character as judged by other people

séance (SAY-ahnss)—a meeting at which people try to make contact with the dead

skeptic (SKEP-tik)—someone who doubts or questions beliefs

spiritualism (SPIHR-uh-choo-uh-li-zuhm)—a religion based on the belief that people can speak to the spirits of the dead

theory (THEE-ur-ee)—an idea that explains something that is unknown

READ MORE

Gagne, Tammy. *Famous Ghosts*. North Mankato, MN: Capstone Press, 2019.

McCollum, Sean. *Handbook to Ghosts, Poltergeists, and Haunted Houses*. North Mankato, MN: Capstone Press, 2017.

Owings, Lisa. *Haunted Houses*. Minneapolis: Bellwether Media, 2019.

INTERNET SITES

Ghost Photography

http://www.bbc.com/future/story/20150629-the-intriguing-history-of-ghost-photography

History of Ghost Stories

https://www.history.com/topics/halloween/historical-ghost-stories

The History of Raynham Hall

http://news.bbc.co.uk/local/norfolk/hi/people_and_places/history/newsid_8058000/8058145.stm

INDEX